James Augustus Hessey

# A Charge Delivered to the Clergy, Churchwardens and Sidesmen of the Archdeaconry of Middlesex

At his Fourth Visitation, (At the end of his Fifth Year), Held at St. Paul's,

Covent Garden, April 29th, 1880

James Augustus Hessey

**A Charge Delivered to the Clergy, Churchwardens and Sidesmen of the Archdeaconry of Middlesex**
*At his Fourth Visitation, (At the end of his Fifth Year), Held at St. Paul's, Covent Garden, April 29th, 1880*

ISBN/EAN: 9783337088446

Printed in Europe, USA, Canada, Australia, Japan

Cover: Foto ©Lupo / pixelio.de

More available books at **www.hansebooks.com**

# SOME QUESTIONS OF THE DAY.

# A CHARGE

DELIVERED TO THE

## Clergy, Churchwardens and Sidesmen

OF THE

## ARCHDEACONRY OF MIDDLESEX,

### At his Fourth Visitation,

(AT THE END OF HIS FIFTH YEAR),

HELD AT

St. Paul's, Covent Garden, April 29th, 1880,

BY

# JAMES AUGUSTUS HESSEY, D.C.L.,

ARCHDEACON OF MIDDLESEX.

LONDON:

THOMAS SCOTT, WARWICK COURT, HOLBORN.

1880.

Several passages in the following Charge were shortened in delivery, and the documents quoted in the course of it were either summarised or wholly omitted. They are printed at length in order that a full record of all matters concerning the recent Election of Proctors may be preserved. An Appendix is given, containing the two Reports of the small Committee appointed by the Bishop to consider the Election of Lay and also of Clerical Representatives at the proposed Diocesan Conference of the Diocese of London. This, in connection with what appeared in the Charges of 1877 and 1878, completes the history of that movement up to the present time.

The Archdeacon takes this opportunity of thanking the Clergy for their very full attendance. He regrets that a mistake on the part of his Apparitor, who, overlooking the clear instructions of the Registrar, summoned some of the Clergy for Wednesday, April 28th, instead of *all* for Thursday, April 29th, caused a little inconvenience. He has desired a copy of his Charge to be sent to all those whose names appear inscribed in his Visitation Book, to all from whom or of whom he has heard that they were unavoidably kept away, and to all whom, through some miscarriage, no Citation had reached. If any who attended, through mistake did not inscribe their names, he will, on hearing from them to that effect, desire copies to be sent to them.

At the Election of Proctors, a Committee of the Incumbents of the Archdeaconry of Middlesex was appointed to consider the subject of the representation of the Parochial Clergy in Convocation, with instructions to place itself in communication with a similar Committee of Incumbents of the other Archdeaconry.

My Reverend Brethren, and my Brethren the Churchwardens and Sidesmen of the Archdeaconry of Middlesex.

The Visitation of the Bishop relieved me from the necessity, or, I should rather say, deprived me of the agreeable duty, of addressing you in your collective capacity last year. I cannot, however, regret this. Our Spiritual Father's well-considered words are more weighty than mine could be even on such subjects as come especially under my cognizance, and they extend to the spiritual as well as to the material organization of the Church. *Our Spiritual Father* —I rejoice to call him by that old-fashioned, but endearing title. His influence with us and over us is founded in paternal sympathies, and in the correlative feelings which these draw forth, not in harsh legal restraint or in grudging submission. Hence I cannot help congratulating you on the recent assertion, by the House of Lords, for our Bishops, of their true relation to the Clergy, which some had supposed to be lost. It is settled, I trust, for ever, that a Bishop is not a mere functionary of the Law, like a process-server compelled to deliver a writ, or like a police-officer bound to arrest a delinquent. He is rather one who before acting, or before permitting action, may exercise discretion, and who may be expected to weigh all the circumstances of any complaint, with tender regard to the welfare of the parties concerned, and to the interests of the Church in general. The settlement of this point has already, in instances which have come to my knowledge, had an excellent effect in bringing back the Clergy to a loyal dependence on the Bishop, and in inducing them to sacrifice their own prepossessions in accordance with his "godly admonitions." The Bishop took occasion in his Charge to encourage his Archdeacons by speaking kindly of "their placing their offices cheerfully and ungrudgingly at his service and that of the Diocese." Though conscious of many shortcomings when I review the five years I have gone in and out amongst you, I have endeavoured to be useful. No Clergyman has appealed to me for personal comfort or counsel—for advice as to Liturgical or Parochial difficulties—for presence at opening his Schools or Mission Chapels, or on Penitential or Festive or Anniversary occasions—for Sermons on all manner of subjects—for Public Induction into his Ministerial position—or for composing of misunderstandings between himself and his Parishioners— or for many other matters—whose wishes I have not met, if I have found it at all possible to do so. And Churchwardens and Sidesmen know that I am always ready to see them and advise with them, to the best of my power, with the assistance of my learned Official Principal. I have experienced a full requital for any sympathy or help which God has permitted me to give in universal welcome by my brethren both Clerical and Lay. I trust I may be henceforth able to render them a more undistracted co-operation, for I have resigned an engagement which occupied a portion of my time, with a view to devoting myself entirely to the business of the Archdeaconry, to the correspondence and other work which it brings upon me, and to the Church Societies which I have to attend. You will pardon my allusion to these points. They have been only noticed because some writers in newspapers have taken upon them to assert that an Archdeacon has really nothing to do, but is induced to finding a reason for his very existence as a Church officer in a sort of πολυπραγμοσύνη, or meddlesome interference with somebody or something or other.

I feel, to my great joy, that I am surrounded by Clergy who

are ever mindful of St. Paul's words to Timothy—men who are walking according "to the former prophecies concerning them," *i.e,* the directions (or prophecies properly so called) of the Holy Spirit spoken concerning them at their original admission to the Ministry by the προφῆται in the Church, and carrying on, as their means of defence and confirmation, the good warfare in which they have engaged as their life-work. And, wherever I go, I find the Laity risen to a consciousness of their Church Membership—finding that they have something to do for God, and doing it. Themselves, their time, their influence, their money, and their prayers are at the disposal of His Church. Instances are not far to seek. But I may mention the names of two who have been recently called to their rest and their reward. One, John Torr, who died just as he was completing the Endowment of a Bishopric for Liverpool, to which he had himself contributed £10,000. The other, for private reasons most dear to me, but on public grounds dear to the whole Church, Philip Cazenove.

The Archdeacon's was originally a purely spiritual office, and was formerly conferred with much solemnity, by investiture of ring and a book, but though many of his functions are still spiritual, many are now temporal. So I proceed without further preface to certain subjects which, though on the border-land of the temporal and spiritual, concern us very much as to the exercise of our spiritual office. Some of them have for good or for evil been already before Parliament—and some of them are likely to be before it. Others are scarcely within the scope of legislation—but are matters of internal ecclesiastical polity. You will understand that what I say is not intended to suggest difficulties, but to state clearly difficulties that exist, and, if possible, to indicate solutions of them.

These matters are :—

(1.) The legalizing of Marriage with a Wife's Sister.

(2.) The Marriage of parties, one or other of which has been divorced.

(3.) The maintenance of the fabrics of our Churches, and the providing for the expenses of Divine Service.

(4.) The seeking out of children to be baptized.

(5.) The right of persons to be married in a Church which is not strictly their Parish Church, and the legal technicalities, more or less affecting the Clergy, which beset the subject of the celebration of Marriages generally.

(6.) The letting, or appropriation, or absolute freedom of seats in Churches; questions which are greatly complicated by the shifting of population.

(7.) The Reform of Convocation.

(8.) The progress of the movement for a Diocesan Conference for the Diocese of London.

(9.) Our duty towards the more destitute parts of the Diocese.

(10.) The condition of the Sunday Question, and the attitude which the Clergy should assume in reference to it.

I will treat of the first two of these together.

## I., II.

It is, I believe, indisputable that a great deal of the recent trouble which we have had as to matters of Ritual, to which I only allude here for the purpose of illustration, has been produced by an impression that certain Courts have only a temporal foundation, and are not qualified, either in their origin or in the appointment or qualifications of their Judges, to decide in matters spiritual. I am not pronouncing on the correctness of this impression, but merely stating that it exists. Whether rightly entertained or no, it is widely spread, and has led to what appears to be, if not an opposition to the law of the land, yet an opposition to the exposition of it emanating from these Courts. (Of course I am aware that such expositions have been objected to on other grounds—such as want of historical knowledge, erroneous setting forth of facts, considerations of expediency being admitted which would not have been admitted in matters purely temporal—but I am concerned with principles rather than with incidental considerations.) Well, an analogous state of things is observable in reference to the second of my two questions, in consequence of actual legislation, and may be feared in reference to the first, if the agitation of those who have already broken the law of the Church and the law of the land is permitted to attain its object.

As to the Marriage of Divorced Persons. You will recollect that, when the Divorce Act was passed, an unhappy compromise was entered into in order to conciliate opponents. The Incumbent of a Parish is not obliged to marry such persons, but he is compelled to allow another Clergyman to marry them in his Church. Well, we will suppose that he feels strongly on the point, and, feeling strongly, has told his Parishioners that he does not consider such a Marriage to be lawful in the sight of God—in fact, that he holds it to be no Marriage at all. But the persons live in his Parish, and present themselves at the Holy Communion. Being, as he holds them to be, not married, he declines to admit them to that ordinance—"as notorious and open evil livers." They appeal, we will further suppose, to the Law Courts, and obtain a decision that they are married, and do not come under this category. What is then the Incumbent's position? I do not know that such a dispute has ever been carried to the bitter end. But I do know that such a case has arisen—that the opinion of eminent Counsel was taken upon it—that it was advised most confidently that the Incumbent would be cast, if it were tried at law—and that collision has only been avoided by the prudence or the timidity of the Incumbent, or by reluctance of the parties to court publicity and have their former lives discussed anew. It cannot, however, be imagined that things will always be kept so quiet. Some day or other, collision must take place between the obligation to obey conscience and to obey temporal law.

It may, however, be said that the Church has ruled nothing absolutely as to the Marriage of Divorced Persons, and that such a scruple, however widely spread, is of private interpretation ; and, moreover, that before the Divorce Act, the temporal power was allowed to override the spiritual, by permitting the Marriage of such persons in particular instances, the only difference being that greater obstacles were thrown in the way. This is true, but it does not remove the stress on the minds of conscientious Clergy, or the continual fear that now such Marriages are legalised by wholesale, they may any day be placed in the dilemma supposed.

It seems to be our duty to petition for a removal of any obligation to allow such Marriages with the offices of the Church, and also of obligation to admit persons to the Holy Communion who have not been married in the Church's pale. For be it observed, the removal of such obligations would not, since the repeal of the Tests and Corporation Acts, deprive any one of temporal privileges, which were dependent upon the reception of the Holy Communion, but would simply relieve the consciences of the Clergy.

It may, however, be said, that it will be very difficult to get such a measure of relief passed through Parliament. Granted. And therefore it is, that setting aside other cogent reasons upon which I have dwelt on former occasions, I would earnestly deprecate the legislative sanction of Marriage with a Deceased Wife's Sister. Such a Marriage is forbidden by the " Table of Kindred and Affinity," wherein whosoever are related are forbidden by Scripture and our laws to marry together." In accordance with this the issue of such a Marriage has been declared by the highest tribunal, that of the House of Lords, to be illegitimate, and incapable of sharing an inheritance under the general designation of children of a testator. No ignorance of the law can be pleaded—in fact the greatest care has been taken by parties desirous of contracting it to evade the law. And it cannot be pleaded, as might be in the case of divorced persons marrying, that they deserve condonation because Marriage is a life of amendment. They are taking their first wrong step, not retracing a wrong step. Already the agitation has done harm, and shaken the sanctity of the relation between a man and his wife and his wife's sister. Already inconvenient preludes to what would occur have been witnessed. Such for instance as persons persuading the Clergy to admit them to the Holy Communion, to the distress of many devout Church people, or resorting to Churches where they are not known. We should, therefore, surely, pause, before we sanction a measure which would add to the embarrassments already existing from contrariety, real or supposed, of the Law of the Land to the Law of Scripture and of the Church.

I have noticed the above objections to sanctioning such Marriages, because I think we ought to look forward to results more carefully than we did at the time when the Divorce Act was passed, and because also I do not remember to have seen the question distinctly regarded under this aspect.

## III.

An embarrassment which is much felt by Churchwardens, now that a Church Rate, though it may be voted in Vestry, cannot be legally enforced, is not, indeed, *in pari materiâ*, but it exhibits an analogous instance of conflict between a duty and the possibility of its performance. The Churchwardens are bound to keep their Church in fitting repair. Previously to the Braintree decision, it was always supposed that they had a right to demand funds from the Parishioners for that purpose. That decision rudely dispelled the illusion of centuries— and the Act which followed it declared, authoritatively, that there should be no grounds for entertaining such an illusion in

future. Still the obligation upon themselves, as men interested
n their Parish Churches, remained—and they felt that they
might at any moment be told that they should not have undertaken a duty which they could not perform, or that having
undertaken it they should perform it at their own cost.
This position is so obviously unjust, as well as so inconvenient,
that the wonder is that persons are found willing to undertake
the office of Churchwarden at all.

Happily this is the case as a rule. In richer places there are
almost always found men who are sufficiently attached to their
Church to help their Clergyman in the hard task which might
otherwise fall upon him, always unfairly, but it is to be
regretted in some cases legally, of keeping up the fabric of the
Church and meeting the expenses of its Services. Sometimes a
voluntary rate has been levied—sometimes subscriptions have
been raised in the Parish—and in many instances, the truer
method has been adopted of meeting these difficulties by
Offertories in the Church itself. There are also some ancient
Parochial Districts in which funds exist for the purposes
designated. Still, many Parishes exist in which Churches are
going out of repair and Services are inadequately conducted, for
want of funds, and for want of opulent persons to contribute
funds—and the number of such Parishes is increasing yearly.
What remedy can be found for this? And on what analogy
can we justify our demand for it?

A Royal Commission has recently reported that there are
considerable Ecclesiastical funds attached to Parishes in the
City which are absolutely not wanted there, and which might
be applied in aid of the erection or repair of Churches, or
generally for the relief of the spiritual wants of the poorer
parishes, within the Metropolitan area. The Commissioners
recommend that such an application should take place. Let
us petition Parliament to that effect. We may surely adduce
the precedent of the re-distribution of Cathedral and Episcopal property. We may urge that City Churches, not

required, have been pulled down—and their endowments and the money received for their sites diverted to the building and endowment of Churches in districts to which the population of the City has migrated. And we may urge also that if the whole of the Metropolitan area is equitably placed on the same basis for Poor Rates, a similar course of action is not inequitable in reference to repair of Churches where the funds are strictly Ecclesiastical. It is true that a special branch of the Bishop of London's Fund has been recently established for the purpose of aiding poor Churches—but, so great has been the pressure of new work, the result has been by no means commensurate with the extent or depth of the want. I should recommend you to read carefully the elaborate Report of the Commission. It is full of interest. And I would have you remember that even in the West and North of London there are many Churches, either actually in need, or likely, at no distant date, to be in need, of the aid which may thus, by timely representation, be permanently secured.

## IV.

I have only one word to say on the subject of Baptisms. It has been alleged that the Clergy do not sufficiently seek out children to be baptized. I do not believe this for a moment. But I have received an important return from Archdeacon Jennings, the Incumbent of the Mother Church of St. John the Evangelist, Westminster, now divided into six Parishes, which may show how many of the children registered our Clergy baptize into the Church, in a district where Roman Catholic efforts are diligently made to secure proselytes to that communion, and which Cardinal Wiseman professed to claim for his own. An average such as it presents is an answer to many cavils—and an encouragement to similar exertions, if there are any Parishes to which they can possibly apply. I set it forth at length for your perusal. It embraces the last four years.

## "PARISH OF ST. JOHN THE EVANGELIST, WESTMINSTER.

### *"Population* (1871), 38,470.

"Number of births returned by the Civil Registrar, and of baptisms registered during the years 1876, 1877, 1878, and 1879, in the six Churches situate within the boundary of the old Parish :—

|  | 1876. | 1877. | 1878. | 1879. |
|---|---|---|---|---|
| " Births | 1,258 | 1,272 | 1,205 | 1,109 |
| St. John's Church | 303 | 344 | 317 | 311 |
| St. Mary's | 172 | 156 | 131 | 137 |
| St Stephen's | 168 | 222 | 176 | 177 |
| St. Matthew's | 130 | 103 | 113 | 96 |
| Holy Trinity | 129 | 130 | 140 | 148 |
| St. James the Less | 64 | 67 | 101 | 77 |
| Baptisms | 966 | 1,022 | 978 | 946 |

"JOHN JENNINGS,

" *March,* 1880."     " *Rural Dean.*

## V.

The next points which I have set down for remark relate to the perplexing position of the Clergy of regularly constituted District Parishes which have been formed, by subdivision and re-subdivision, and also by the method of Consolidated Chapelries out of older Parishes, in reference to Marriages—and the legal technicalities more or less affecting the Clergy which beset the subject of Marriages generally—I would dwell most on the former of these.

The position of which complaint is made has been stated to me in this wise.

" There are three Parishes, which for distinction sake, I will name *A. B. C.*"

" *A.* is a Mother Parish, one of the oldest in London, which, though for Ecclesiastical purposes it has been subdivided again and again, remains, for Civil purposes, one and undivided, with its central Vestry, and other Parochial powers and machinery."

" *B.* is a District Parish taken out of that Mother Parish

more than thirty years ago, and formed into a separate Parish for all Ecclesiastical purposes."

" *C.* is a ' Consolidated Chapelry ' formed out of portions taken from *B.*, and two other Parishes *D.* and *E.*"

" Now I find that persons residing in *B.* claim to be married in the Parish Church of *A.*, and I believe that their claim is supported by the Chancellor of the Diocese. But there is a constant difficulty about Marriages between *C.* and *B.*

" The Vicar of *B.* has tried to meet this difficulty—

" (1.) By offering to receive Marriages from that portion of *C.* (the Consolidated Chapelry), which was originally in *B.*, in his Church, and to give to the Vicar of *C.* one half of the Marriage fees. This has not been a welcome proposal.

" (2.) By standing on his (presumed) right to receive persons to be married in his Church from the part of *C.*, which used to be in his Parish, whenever a strong wish to this effect is expressed, though he will not himself put any pressure upon such persons to be married in his Church.

" Now the two questions which I should like to have settled are these—

" 1*st*. Whether the right of persons resident in *B.* to be married in the Church of the Mother Parish *A.* is equally the right of persons resident in *C.* (that portion of it, I mean, which belonged originally to *B.*), to be married in Parish Church *B.*?

" 2*nd*. What is understood by a ' Consolidated Chapelry,' and whether it is to all intents and purposes the same as a District Parish ?

" May I also ask whether you think the proposal to give one half of the Marriage fees, in the case mentioned above, a fair one ?"

I wish I could answer these questions fully. But I must honestly confess that they cannot be satisfactorily solved except by Act of Parliament.

I will give, however, such answers as I can.

*1st.* A Consolidated Chapelry, if regularly constituted, is to all intents a District Parish. Therefore, whatever rights the inhabitants of a District Parish lose, or whatever rights they retain, those same rights are lost or retained by the inhabitants of the Consolidated Chapelry.

But, *2ndly,* What are these rights?

I told you, in 1878 (with the qualification, that others think otherwise), that it is the opinion of my learned Official Principal that Banns of Marriages should be published not in the Church of the Mother Parish, but in the Church of the District in which one or both of the parties proposes to contract a Marriage reside. For the obvious intention of publication of Banns is that clandestine or unlawful Marriages may be prevented by the knowledge of relations and neighbours. In the same way Marriages by License should, in strictness, (for a License is only a permission to dispense with the formality of Banns), be celebrated in the District Parish Church to which at least one of the parties belong, and not in the Parish Church. The fees would, of course, go to the Minister and Clerk of the Church in which the Marriage is celebrated—at least when all the conditions of separation as well as of legal constitution of the District Parish have been complied with. This *dictum* would carry with it the general principle that the Parishioners of the District Parish are not entitled to the ministrations of the Mother Parish. The Incumbent of the District Parish is their legal Minister; and it would follow that the only Parishioners of the now diminished Mother Parish would be those who are left in it after legal separation and constitution of the District Parish have taken place.

It is difficult to conceive that the legalizing of District Parishes for the celebration of Marriages therein could have had any other meaning than this. But another legal principle steps in, that persons do not lose Civil privileges by any Act,

unless it is expressly declared in that Act that they are to
lose it. On this principle it is, I suppose, that the Chancellor
issues Marriage Licenses for persons residing in what *was*
the Parish of *A.*, though now residing in District Parishes,
to be married in the Mother Church *A*. His interpretation
is, I conceive, authoritative, and, hard as it is upon the
Ministers and Clerks of the District Parishes to have their
Parishioners diverted from them, or their sometimes scanty
surplice fees paid elsewhere, I must conclude that the Parishioners of *B.* may be married by License, and, if so, by
Banns, in the Parish Church of *A*. And so, by parity of
reasoning, that Parishioners in that part of *C.* which has been
taken out of *B.* may be married in the Parish Church of *B.*,
and, indeed, of *A.* also. And I see nothing to prevent those
of *D.* and *E.* who were taken out of other Parishes, and
made contributors to the Consolidated Chapelry *C.*, from
asserting, in a similar way, their civil right to be married in
their respective old Mother Churches.

All this is very perplexing and confusing, and, I am
persuaded, is really contrary to what was intended by the
constitution of District Parishes. It is also hard upon the
Clergy in the way that I have stated. I do not think that a
proposal to divide the Fees is at all a satisfactory one. No
one should be called upon to surrender remuneration for work
that he has actually performed; and no one likes to receive
remuneration for what he does not do. Besides, isolated
instances of such an arrangement would produce invidious
comparisons between the liberality of one Incumbent and
that of another, and misunderstandings which would be
stigmatized as disputes about Fees.

I can suggest no remedy except, for the present, dis-
couragement, so far as is possible, of Marriages elsewhere
than in the actual Parish Church of one of the parties;
and, prospectively, the hope of a well-considered Act of

Parliament, for which we should petition, and which I understand has been long in view, to put these and certain other matters connected with Marriages on some other footing. We certainly need a reformation of various abuses —the fiction, for instance, of a temporary lodging in a Parish to enable one of the parties to apply for a License in order to be married as a resident. We need to be told by authority whether persons may be married in the Church whose Banns have not been published there, but whose intention has been notified in a Registrar's office. We need liberty to decline to marry persons who are not Christians. We need that it should be set forth clearly that Banns published in Churches of the Episcopal Church of Scotland, or in Chapels of the Continent, are not producible as sufficiently published for Marriages in England. We need protection to young women who marry aliens, and whose Marriages, when they reach their husband's country, may be found illegal by the laws of that country ; and many other needs of the same character might be specified—to say nothing of the hardship on the Clergy produced by the Divorce Act, which I have already mentioned.

No Government has hitherto had leisure or inclination to take up so complicated a subject; and we of the Clergy are sometimes inclined to fear that whatever remedy may be proposed will be found to be worse than the disease. But surely this is a faint-hearted and timorous policy, and has led to many evils already. I trust that is not true of the Church of England, which Livy pronounced of Rome :— " *Ad hæc tempora, quibus nec vitia nostra, nec remedia pati possumus, perventum est.*" The following is a *programme* of a Bill of which notice was given by Mr. Blennerhassett in the late Parliament. It does not meet all the points of which complaints is or may be made, and I do not see the necessity of the provision mentioned under the fourth head. But, if introduced in the new Parliament, it may be either amended, or made a stock on which to engraft other necessary enactments. Its main provisions are:—

(1.) Relief of the Clergy from the obligation of having anything whatever to do with the Marriage of Divorced persons.

(2.) Relief of the Nonconformists from the obligation of having the Registrar present at their Marriages.

(3.) Giving Church people more liberty with regard to the Church in which the Marriage is to be solemnized.

(4.) Extension of the hours in which Marriage may be solemnized.

(5.) Validating certain Marriages which would be invalid for wilful non-compliance with forms, although the Marriage may have been actually solemnized, and the parties have believed themselves to be legally married, and have lived together twenty years.

And we are given to understand by the draftsman of this Bill that it is not proposed to abolish Banns, but only to make one of the persons intending Marriage, when he "puts up" the Banns, sign a written notice and declaration, instead of merely giving a verbal notice. This, he thinks, will assist in preventing false statements and mistakes. He adds, "If Banns were done away with it would be necessary to provide that a book, containing notices of Marriage, should lie at the Clergyman's house for any one to see. And I doubt whether the Clergy would approve of such an arrangement."

---

## VI.

I now come to a subject which, considering its difficulty, I would fain avoid, but which, from its intrinsic importance, as well from the practical questions which it involves, and in which Churchwardens and Sidesmen are concerned, I may not pass over.

I allude to what is so much—and in the abstract with so much reason—agitated for in the present day: the freedom and openness of sittings, or rather kneelings, in the House of God.

There is no doubt in the world upon two or three points: that the Parishioners are entitled, in the first instance, to be accommodated; that it is necessary, in order that decorum should be observed, that the Churchwardens and Sidesmen

B

should see that they are duly accommodated; and that by the word *duly* should be understood that they should be able to worship with their families, and not be scattered here and there, so that the domestic union would be broken through.

These objects, it may be believed, were originally attained by the Churchwardens and Sidesmen being in attendance before the Service commenced, to perform their office of allotting seats, and by the Parishioners themselves being so regular in their coming to the Church, as to be shown to seats without noise and without interruption.

Regularity on both parts produced an appropriation of seats, for persons liked to worship, Sunday after Sunday, in the same spot; and if no selfishness or exclusiveness had stept in, and there had been, in all places, abundance of room, there would not have been much to complain of.

But these ugly visitants did step in, and the officers found it easier to assign groups of seats, once for all, than to be in attendance always to do their duty. Thus groups of seats took the form of huge pews or pens, which were allotted to persons *in perpetuum*, and whether they and their families came to Church in good time, or not at all, were reserved to them. The poor were gradually thrust into the more obscure or less eligible portions of the Church, and so in many places ceased to attend altogether. And, especially in large towns, where the population had outgrown the dimensions of the Church, and where the income of the Living was small, or money was not forthcoming to make repairs of the edifice, pews were let for hire, and were locked up* in their renter's absence, or even considered matters of sale or inheritance. Besides this, there grew up a system of pews appropriated by faculty or prescription, and of attachment of

* There is, I am sorry to say, one Church in the Diocese, that of Staines, built in 1827, under a Special Act of Parliament, 7 and 8 George IV., cap. cvii., where holders of pews have a freehold interest in them, and have refused to allow them to be opened for a third free Service, even when they themselves are not present.

pews to a certain house, which was utterly destructive of the principles that the Church belongs to all, and that persons who will not come to worship in it should not prevent those who will.

In great cities, like London and its suburbs, the evils are complicated by the very remedies which have been suggested or adopted.

Churches and chapels have been built, in which pew-letting is the system, and in which there is either no accommodation for the poor, or very little accommodation, and that of the worst kind. And since Church Rates have been irrecoverable by law, Churchwardens have sometimes, even in old Parish Churches, entered upon an understanding with the holders of pews or seats, somewhat of the following character. " You, to whom such and such a good seat is allotted, are bound by a sort of honourable understanding to contribute so much to Church expenses. You, to whom a less eligible seat, so much ;" and so on to the end of the chapter, which frequently arrives without any room being found for the poor. Then, again, covenants with the Incorporated Society for Building and Repairing Churches and Chapels, or other Societies, have been frequently forgotten. Parts of the Church which were to be free have been let, and the poor are placed, on various excuses, in parts of the Church where they cannot see or hear.

No wonder that this state of things excited the attention of the Founders of the Free and Open Church Association, as it is called. If I have not actually joined their ranks, it is not because I do not sympathise with their general objects, but, because, as it appears to me, they do not exercise quite so much forbearance and discrimination, as is required by the difficulties of the Church's position in the present day.

In Country Churches, the solution of knots in the matter is comparatively easy. The pews, so aesthetically as well as so religiously unsightly, have only to be swept away, and

B 2

replaced by open benches; families may still have their appropriated seats—for I would respect the family feeling—if they are in Church a few minutes before the Service commences; and if the Churchwardens are in attendance to see that under fulfilment of this condition they have them, and at its non-fulfilment, fill up their places by admitting others to them — all are accommodated and none are aggrieved. Here and there, perhaps, a holder of a tall-sided faculty or prescriptive pew, insists on his right to retain his huge construction. But he may be let alone. Bear with him—leave him alone in his isolated selfishness.

> " Si defendere delictum quam vertere malles
> Nullum ultra verbum aut operam insumebat inanem
> Quin sine rivali teque et tua solus amares,"

said Horace, of a different matter indeed, but using words much to the vexed Clergyman's purpose. If he will not yield, possibly his successor will. Perhaps he may yield bye and bye.*

I have everywhere pressed the doctrine that in old Parish Churches payment for seats, or even such *quasi* payment as is implied in the so-called honourable understanding I have already mentioned, is absolutely illegal. But I cannot join in an undiscriminating cry, especially in London, against appropriation of seats to regular attendants at Church, or against all letting of seats, or against the legalizing of such

---

* This may be shown by the following anecdote. A Clergyman, not of this Diocese, reseated his Church. One holder of a faculty pew would not fall in with the plan. The Clergyman let him alone. When everything else had been completed, the great pew was left standing, and very hideous it was. The holder one day brought a friend into the Church, and pointing to the pew said, " There, our Parson with his new-fangled views wanted to level my pew to the rest. I stood on my legal position. Don't you think I am right? " " Well," said his friend, " you may have law, and right on your side ; I will not discuss that. But the enclosure is singularly like that for strayed animals, which we call the Pound. I should not like to be a subject for it. But that is a matter of taste." The mortified owner said nothing. A few days after he called upon the Clergyman with " There, I have asserted my right. And now you may reduce the pew as you please." So the thing was done. The moral is let us, proceed gently and without haste or invective.

letting, by an application of the remnant of the Million Fund. I will tell you why.

If a Church happens to be what is called a popular one, either from the nature of the Services or from the ability of the Clergyman, a crowd of people will invade it, and the regular attendants or Parishioners will be ousted, and their families separated.

In many neighbourhoods unless some seats are let there is at present no means of supporting a Clergyman for large districts where the population has entirely outrun the existing accommodation. There is no prospect of endowment—and Churches would hardly have been built at all, unless resort had been made to the much-vituperated Million Fund in order to legalize letting some of the seats.

Does it follow therefore, that scandal should be allowed to exist—that in Churches, whether of old or of new foundation, with seats appropriated to Parishioners or to Renters, the doors should be besieged before the Service commences, so that the regular worshippers cannot enter in, or the aisles noisily thronged with those who have no regular seats, until a very important part of the Service has been got through.

I answer emphatically, No. Let us get rid at once of the practice of reserving seats to any one beyond five minutes before the bell stops.

Let the Churchwardens retain their power which they possess, under the Ordinary, of appropriating seats to individuals and even to families, and let the right of Renters of seats, (where this is a necessity), be preserved.

But let no seat be appropriated or let, without the condition above mentioned. And let the Churchwardens be in attendance, and, if they want help, Sidesmen and other Church-helpers will be ready to assist them in enforcing this condition. It will be perfectly easy to do this eventually. In the old Churches the Churchwardens will only be resuming their power and exercising it diligently every Sunday, instead of indolently once for all. In the new Churches, they can exercise it also, if a notice is placed up at the Church-door, or fixed in the seats themselves, that such is the condition of tenure. Where seats are rented, there should, in addition to this, be a memorandum to that effect, printed on the receipt for payment. By degrees persons would find that it is just as easy to come to Church five minutes before the time, as five minutes after. And I am persuaded that, by degrees also, feelings of exclusiveness will give way, and thoughts for those to whom especially the Gospel is preached will grow up. Besides this, however, there might be Services at which every seat is absolutely free, and at which the poor might be especially encouraged to attend.

My Brethren of the Clergy, and my Lay Brethren the Churchwardens and Sidesmen, will pardon my free speaking on this matter. And if these words reach the Laity generally, I trust they will second the efforts of those who, while they respect rights, feel bound to inculcate duties.

## VII.

Another subject upon which considerable interest has been felt amongst us is the Reform of Convocation, so far at least as the adequate Representation of the Parochial Clergy of this Diocese is concerned.

You will remember that, in my Charge of 1878, I recounted to you, with some particularity, the changes which have already taken place in the constitution of the Convocation of the Northern Province. I then proposed to you that " we should petition our Bishop to urge upon the Archbishop of Canterbury that Archdeaconries should, as in the Province of York, be made the basis of the Representation of the Parochial Clergy, and that at least two Proctors should be elected and sit for each Archdeaconry."

And I urged that, among other advantages of this arrangement, would be the rectification of the proportion of

Parochial Proctors as compared with the official element of Deans and Archdeacons and Proctors of Cathedrals.

My ultimate design in saying this was to promote the efficiency of Convocation, by making it really representative of the Clergy. My immediate object was to obtain a fair representation of the Clergy of our own Diocese.

I do not think that I mentioned enlargement of the constituency, by allowing other licensed Priests than Incumbents, under certain limitations of course, to have votes ; but I did mention the desirableness of allowing them to vote for Members of a proposed Diocesan Conference for London. I need hardly assure you, however, that such a measure would have had my thorough approbation.

You did not, I regret, adopt my suggestion of addressing the Bishop. (Perhaps I may observe, by the way, that your not having done so is somewhat due to the want of that Diocesan organization which a Diocesan Conference, which virtually includes a Diocesan Synod, or a Diocesan Synod pure and simple would have effected.) The result was that an election of Proctors for a new Convocation came upon us without our having made our convictions and wishes thoroughly and formally known.

But though we were, I think, unwisely silent, it would seem that the hardship of our case did not altogether escape the Archbishop of Canterbury. Unprepared as His Grace was to adopt the precedent of the Archbishop of York, as to the admission of more Parochial Proctors for each Diocese, and, I suppose, more unprepared still to allow votes to others than Incumbents, he issued the following letter. His feeling, no doubt, was, first, that the Incumbents ought to be induced to take more general and lively interest in the elections than they have done heretofore ; and, secondly, that they should in all cases be *directly* represented—namely, by the Incumbents most approved by them being selected by the Bishop. Accordingly, he issued the following letter to every one of his comprovincials. It is dated—

"Lambeth Palace, *S.E.*,

"My dear Lord,                                    "20th March, 1880.

"I expect within a few days to be commanded by her Majesty the Queen to issue, through the Bishop of London, (as Dean of the Province), the writs for the election of a new Convocation for Canterbury.

"I would venture to suggest to your lordship two improvements in the mode of selecting Proctors to represent your Diocese in the Lower House which might, I think, with advantage be made at the coming elections.

"1. I would commend to you a system of ascertaining the wishes of the Clergy by voting papers, which has already been adopted in more than one Diocese. According to this system, the beneficed Clergy appoint a small central body of their own number, to whom the voting papers are returned, and this central body, adhering to the old form, afterwards *meets* and *elects* the candidates for whom the largest number of votes has been recorded.

"2. I would also submit whether it is not desirable in cases in which, from old prescription, the Bishop has the right of selecting, as Proctors, two out of several names submitted to him by the Clergy, that the Bishop should waive this right and nominate the candidates for whom the largest number of votes has been recorded.

"Believe me to be, my dear Lord,

"Your faithful servant and brother,

"A. C. CANTUAR."

It is obvious that two points must have escaped his Grace when he penned this letter. First, that it is necessary that the Incumbents should be cited to elect in the first instance, otherwise the voting papers collected and their result would be due rather to the action of a committee or *caucus*, than to a formal and solemn meeting of the Clergy; secondly, that it would be impossible, seeing that the number of Proctors for each Diocese is by custom limited to two, for the Bishop to give effect to the choice of the Clergy in his Archdeaconries unless the Archdeaconries also are two only. For instance, it could not apply to Rochester, where there are three Archdeaconries, those of Rochester, Southwark, and Kingston-on-Thames. The Bishop of Rochester could not choose the most preferred of every one of his three, and thus one of them must be unrepresented. In like manner, it could not apply to the Diocese of St. Alban's,* where there are also

---

* *See* Appendix, page 43.

three Archdeaconries, those of St. Alban's, Essex and Colchester. And had the Diocese of London still possessed, as it did until 1838, five Archdeaconries—*viz.*, those of Essex, Colchester, and St. Alban's, besides those of London and Middlesex—it would have been utterly inapplicable to it also. If I may judge from the mandates sent out by the Bishop of London previous to that date, which I have carefully perused in the Register, and which are obviously handed down from remote antiquity, each of the five Archdeacons was to see that two good and sufficient Procurators were elected. If, therefore, according to the Archbishop's recommendation, the Bishop were to select those for whom the largest number of votes has been recorded, five would have had to be sent up from the Diocese of London. For, as the Archbishop puts it, the Clergymen who received the largest number of votes, would have to be taken. There would be no possibility of comparing the numbers given in distinct Archdeaconries, so as to carry out the suggestion.

Still, as it might apply to the Diocese of London under its present circumstances, the Bishop of London, in order to meet, as far as he thought he could at present, the wishes of his Clergy, issued the following letter to each of his Archdeacons. I give it at length, because, though I have acted upon its suggestions, as to procedure, there are some points in it of considerable importance, from which I am constrained to differ:—

"London House, St. James' Square,
"March 27th, 1880.

"My dear Archdeacon,—I have received a letter from the Archbishop of Canterbury, suggesting the adoption, at the coming election of Proctors for Convocation, of the mode of ascertaining the opinion of the Clergy by means of polling papers.

"You will infer, from a recent conversation we held together, that I entirely concur in His Grace's suggestion. Great weight is no doubt due to the opinion of eminent lawyers, expressed almost with unanimity, that any structural change in the constitution of the Church's Convocation, whether made by extending the constituency or by increasing the number of Proctors, (excepting the increase which takes place necessarily in strict accordance with the old constitution, when a new Diocese or a new Archdeacoury is created), if made without the concurrent authority of the Legislature or of the Crown, would throw serious doubt on the validity of the acts and proceedings of a body thus altered. But no such objection seems to lie against a modification, for the convenience of the Clergy, of the machinery, so to speak, by which their votes are ascertained, which rests on no enactment, and can affect in no way the character or constitution of the body elected.

" You will probably, therefore, think it well to summon the beneficed Clergy of your Archdeaconry on a convenient day to elect, or to nominate for election, Clergymen as Proctors for Convocation. If two only are proposed, the election will be at once concluded. If more than two are duly proposed and seconded, you may adjourn the election to a day to be then named ; and polling papers, containing the names of those proposed, can be at once prepared and sent by post to every Incumbent in your Archdeaconry, with directions to fill and sign them and to return them before or to bring them before a certain hour on the day to which the election was adjourned. The papers can then be opened and examined before yourself and a mover or seconder of each of the candidates. The names of the two Clergymen who receive the highest number of votes, together with the number of votes received by them, will be returned to me.

" I wish the Clergy to be informed that it is my intention to select for Proctor the Clergyman who, in each Archdeaconry, shall receive the largest number of votes, unless informed by that Clergyman himself that he declines to serve.

" I departed from this rule in the case of the Archdeaconry of Middlesex at the last election only because I was told, on what I considered sufficient authority, that the Clergyman whose name stood first was unwilling to be selected to the exclusion of the second, who had sat in the previous Convocation. In future I shall receive any such intimation only from the Clergyman himself. My wish is to give effect to the choice of the Clergy.

" You will, no doubt, remind the Clergy that each is at liberty to give one vote to two of the nominated candidates; but that he cannot give his two votes to the same candidate.

" Yours truly,
" JOHN LONDON."

Such was the Bishop's letter. Immediately following upon the receipt of it, came His Lordship's mandate to me, in which he set forth the tenour of a mandatory letter which he had received from the Archbishop :—

*Seal.*

" JOHN, by Divine Permission, Bishop of London, to Our Beloved in Christ, the Archdeacon of the Archdeaconry of Middlesex, or his Official, Greeting, by virtue and authority of certain Mandatory Letters of the Most Reverend Father in God, Archibald Campbell, by Divine Providence, Archbishop of Canterbury, Primate of all England and Metropolitan, bearing date the twenty-fifth day of March instant; also of a certain Writ or Mandate therein contained of Our Most Gracious Sovereign, Lady Victoria, by the Grace of God of the United Kingdom of Great Britain and Ireland,

Queen Defender of the Faith, and so forth, dated at Westminster the twenty-fourth day of March instant, and in the forty-third year of Her Reign, issued out and directed to the said Most Reverend Father for holding and celebrating a sacred Synod and General Convocation of the Prelates and Clergy of the whole Province of Canterbury, We do peremptorily cite and admonish you the Archdeacon aforesaid, that you cause all and singular the Rectors, Vicars, and others as well exempt as not exempt, having and obtaining Benefices and Ecclesiastical Promotions within the Archdeaconry of Middlesex; and also we enjoin and command you and them that you the Archdeacon aforesaid, personally, and the Clergy of your said Archdeaconry, by two sufficient Procurators lawfully and sufficiently empowered, do appear before the said Most Reverend Father, ARCHIBALD CAMPBELL, Archbishop of Canterbury, or his Substitute, or Commissary, in the Chapter House of the Cathedral Church of Saint Paul, London, on the thirtieth day of April next, or on such other day to which the said Convocation shall on that day be prorogued. Moreover we command you as above that you duly certify to us, or our Vicar General, by your Letters Patent containing the tenor of these Presents, and sealed with your seal, the names of all and singular the persons cited or admonished in this behalf, also the names of the Procurators chosen for the Clergy aforesaid, and everything else that you shall do in and about the premises, on or before the twenty-third day of April next, and without further delay.

"Dated at London, the thirty-first day of March, in the year of Our Lord, One thousand eight hundred and eighty, and in the twelfth year of our Translation.

"(*Signed*) JOHN B. LEE,
"*Registrar.*"

From the latter of these two documents I gathered that I was to return two Procurators to appear before the Archbishop. I found in it no mention whatever of the prescriptive right of the Bishop to select either one out of them, or two out of the four returned from the whole Diocese. This I gained solely from the former of the documents. It was not my business to dispute but simply to obey—and to state what instructions I had received to my Clergy. I did not hold to the distinction made in the Bishop's letter, that alterations in the mode of voting, and waiving of his prescriptive right of selecting, were simply modifications of machinery, while increase in the number of Proctors, and extension of the constituency, were structural changes. I held both classes of alterations to be referable to one and the same category. And I was not at all persuaded that the Archbishop of

Canterbury could not do for the Southern Province something like what the Archbishop of York did some time ago for the Northern Province. Therefore I caused my Citations to be issued as usual, and with them addressed a letter to the Clergy, founded, indeed, upon the Bishop's letter, but only mentioning what he intended to do—how far he intended to depart from the precedent of late years, and how far he intended to abide by it. This is the present Citation—

" No.

#### " ARCHDEACONRY OF MIDDLESEX.

" *Convocation*, 1880.

" *To the Rev.*                                                                                  *of*

*in the County of Middlesex.*

" By VIRTUE of a Process under the Seal of the Archdeaconry Court of Middlesex, issued in compliance with a Mandate of JOHN, by Divine permission Lord Bishop of London, you are hereby cited personally to appear before The Venerable JAMES AUGUSTUS HESSEY, Clerk, Doctor in the Civil Law, Archdeacon of the said Archdeaconry, or the Worshipful ALFRED WADDILOVE, Doctor in the Civil Law, Official of the said Archdeacon, or his Surrogate, in the Great Room of the National Society for Promoting the Education of the Poor in the Principles of the Established Church, in the Broad Sanctuary, Westminster, in the County of Middlesex, on Thursday, the fifteenth day of April instant, at the hour of Two o'clock in the Afternoon, then and there to Nominate and Elect two sufficient Procurators to appear before the Most Reverend Father in God, ARCHIBALD CAMPBELL, by Divine Providence Lord Archbishop of Canterbury, or his Substitute or Commissary, in the Chapter House of the Cathedral Church of St. Paul, London, on the thirtieth day of April instant, or on such other day to which Convocation shall on that day be prorogued.

" W. L. HARVEY,

" *Apparitor to the said Official.*

" 3rd April, 1880.

" The Registry of the Archdeaconry of Middlesex,

" 10, Godliman Street, Doctors' Commons, *E.C.*

" 3rd April, 1880."

This is my own letter—

" 41, Leinster Gardens,

" Hyde Park, *W*.

" April 3rd, 1880.

" Reverend and dear Brother,

" It is my duty to send you notice for the election of two Proctors for the Archdeaconry of Middlesex, of whom one will be selected by the Bishop, to serve in the approaching Convocation ; and I wish at the same time to give you such information as is required in reference to an alteration which will take place in the mode and circumstances of the election.

"I regret that I am unable to tell you that the constituency of the Proctors to be elected is to be extended on the present occasion, or that the number of Proctors assigned to the Diocese is to be increased. His Grace the President does not yet see his way to these important changes, though I hope they may be effected bye and bye; but he has sanctioned the method of taking the votes of the Clergy by means of voting papers, to which the Bishop has given his hearty consent.

"The following are the arrangements which I have made :—

"On Thursday, April 15, at two o'clock, I request you and all the beneficed Clergy of the Archdeaconry to meet in the Great Room of the National Society, Westminster, to elect, or to nominate for election, then and there, Clergymen as Proctors for Convocation. If two only are duly proposed and seconded, the election will be at once concluded, and I shall only, if necessary, have a further show of hands, that it may appear clearly which of the two elected is the more approved. The result will be reported to the Bishop. If more than two are duly proposed and seconded, I shall adjourn the election to a future day and hour to be then named. In the interval, polling papers will be prepared, containing the names of the candidates, and will be sent by post to every one of the electors, with directions to fill up and sign them, and to return them before—or bring them on—the day and hour to which the election has been adjourned. I mention the alternative, *bring them on*, because every elector has a right to be personally present at the election.

"The papers will then be opened and examined before myself and a mover or seconder of each of the candidates. The names of the two Clergymen who receive the highest number of votes, together with the numbers of votes received by them respectively, will be reported to the Bishop. The Bishop desires to have this information, because it is his intention to give effect to the deliberate choice of the electors by selecting the Clergyman who shall appear to have been thus most approved by them.

"I think it right to remind you that each elector is at liberty to give one vote to two of the candidates nominated, but that he cannot give his two votes to one candidate.

"Praying that God may direct our course for the good of His Church.

"I am,
"Reverend and dear Brother,
"Yours very truly,
"J. A. HESSEY, D.C.L.,
"*Archdeacon of Middlesex.*

"To the Reverend

I have been asked why I did not issue voting papers before the day proposed for election of Proctors. My reply is very obvious. It was my business to cite the Clergy to appear personally. It was not my business to suppose that they would not appear, or that there would be a division in their opinion. If they did appear and agree, there would be an end of the matter. If however, on the day and hour fixed, they thought or any of them thought, on merely two Candidates being proposed, that their pretensions were not sufficiently known in the Archdeaconry, or that the Meeting was not sufficiently numerous to express the general feeling of the Archdeaconry, a third Candidate had only to be proposed— and then, a convenient day of adjournment having been settled, the general feeling might be ascertained by means of voting papers. I was assured that any other method might possibly invalidate the election. This point was fully considered by the Bishop in consultation with his Archdeacons, and hence the method which I adopted.

Well, our Meeting took place as arranged—a very different one in point of numbers from that described to me by one of our most respected Incumbents, Canon Harvey, who I regret to say is now leaving us, after fifty years spent in the Diocese.

"In my early days," he says, "not above one or two Clergymen, Dr. Spry, Rector of St. Marylebone, Mr. Tyler, Rector of St. Giles, and perhaps a third, ever came to an election of Proctors. We met in the Vestry of St. Paul's, Covent Garden, and the business was despatched in five minutes."

Now, men came, fully convinced of the importance of Convocation even as it is, and fully bent, if it might be, on improving it. There were, at least, one hundred and sixty present.

After Prayers, I addressed a few words to the Meeting stating the circumstances under which it had been called together, and the obviously kind intentions of the Archbishop and the Bishop. The alterations conceded were not, indeed, all that we could desire. They did not do away

with the unreality of which we complained. They did not
set the representation of the Parochial Clergy on a perfectly
satisfactory footing. Still, I urged, they were movements in
the right direction, and should be accepted with cordiality.
I am happy to say that you agreed with me, and that a
kindly and genial tone pervaded the proceedings. Four
Candidates were duly proposed and seconded, and I
adjourned the Election to Thursday, April 22nd, between
eleven and twelve in the forenoon, in the Board Room of
the National Society. Before that time, I informed you,
polling papers, of which I showed you the form, might be
addressed to me by post at that place, or delivered personally at that time and place by the Electors. I announced
also that no one except the scrutineers, a proposer or
seconder of each of the Candidates, was then obliged to be
present, but that any one might be present if he chose.
The Meeting was then dismissed with the Benediction.

The following documents were issued:—

"41, Leinster Gardens,
"Hyde Park, W.,
"April 15th, 1880.
" Reverend and dear Sir,
" You are requested to sign the polling paper on the other side and to
return it by post to me at the office of the National Society, Broad Sanctuary,
Westminster, or to bring it with you to the Board Room thereof, on Thursday,
the 22nd of April instant, between the hours of eleven and twelve o'clock.
" I am,
" Reverend and dear Sir,
" Yours very faithfully,
"J. A. HESSEY, D.C.L.,
"*Archdeacon of Middlesex.*

" *N.B.*—Each Incumbent may vote for any *two* of the Candidates; but he
must not give more than one vote to either.

" To the Reverend

## "ARCHDEACONRY OF MIDDLESEX.

### " *Convocation,* 1880.

### "VOTING PAPER.

| 1 | The Rev. George Howard Wilkinson, M.A., Vicar of St. Peter's, Eaton Square. | . |
|---|---|---|
| 2 | The Rev. George Hewitt Hodson, M.A., Vicar of Enfield. | |
| 3 | The Rev. William Cadman, M.A., Rector of Trinity, St. Marylebone. | |
| 4 | The Rev. James Fleming, B.D., Vicar of St. Michael, Chester Square, and Canon Residentiary of York. | |

" I hereby vote for the Clergyman (or Clergymen) against whose name, (or names,) I have placed my initials.

" Signed,..............................................................

" Incumbent of..........................................................

On the appointed day and hour, I held the adjourned Meeting. It was to a certain extent formal, the only persons necessarily in attendance being myself and the scrutineers, and my legal advisers, but several Incumbents also were present, as they had a full right to be. Mr. Wilkinson and Mr. Cadman were found, on examination of the polling papers, to be elected, and were therefore returned under my official seal, to the Bishop.

The form of return was as follows:—

*To the Right Reverend Father in God,* John, *by Divine Permission* Lord Bishop of London.

"We, James Augustus Hessey, Clerk, Doctor in the Civil Law, Archdeacon of Middlesex, do with all due reverence and obedience certify your Lordship that having lately received your Mandate of the tenour following to wit:

*(Here is set out the Bishop of London's Mandate verbatim.)*

" We did by virtue thereof cause all and singular the Rectors, Vicars, and others, as well exempt as not exempt, having and obtaining Benefices

*Seal.*

and Ecclesiastical Promotions within our Archdeaconry aforesaid, to be cited and monished to appear before Us or the Worshipful ALFRED WADDILOVE, Doctor in the Civil Law, our Official, or his Surrogate, in the Great Room of the National Society for Promoting the Education of the Poor in the Principles of the Established Church, in the Broad Sanctuary, Westminster, on Thursday, the 15th day of April instant, at the hour of two o'clock in the afternoon, then and there to nominate and elect two sufficient Procurators to appear before the Most Reverend Father in God, ARCHIBALD CAMPBELL, by Divine Providence Lord Archbishop of Canterbury, or his Substitute or Commissary, in the Chapter House of the Cathedral Church of St. Paul, London, on the 30th day of April instant, or to such other day to which Convocation shall on that day be prorogued; and we do annex hereto a list or Schedule of the names of the said Rectors, Vicars, and others so cited, and the Clergy then present rightly and duly proceeding to the election of two sufficient Proctors as aforesaid, did nominate for election the Rev. George Howard Wilkinson, M.A., Vicar of St. Peter's, Eaton Square; the Rev. George Hewitt Hodson, M.A., Vicar of Enfield; the Rev. William Cadman, M.A., Rector of Trinity, St. Marylebone; and the Rev. James Fleming, B.D., Vicar of St. Michael, Chester Square, and Canon Residentiary of York; and We did then adjourn the Election or Poll until Thursday, the 22nd day of April instant, at the hour of 11 o'clock in the forenoon, at the Office of the National Society aforesaid, and on the said 22nd day of April instant the said Clergy having recorded their votes, and the same having been carefully scrutinized and the numbers ascertained, We did find that the Clergy aforesaid had manifested by their votes and did choose the said Rev. George Howard Wilkinson and the Rev. William Cadman as two sufficient Proctors for the Clergy of the whole Archdeaconry of Middlesex aforesaid, to appear for them before the Most Reverend Father in God, ARCHIBALD CAMPBELL, by Divine Providence Lord Archbishop of Canterbury, or his Substitute or Commissary, in the Chapter House of the Cathedral Church of St. Paul, London, on the 30th day of April instant, or on such other day to which Convocation shall on that day be prorogued. In witness whereof We have caused our Seal to be affixed to these presents.

"Dated at London this 23rd day of April, 1880.

"(*Signed*) CYRUS WADDILOVE,

"*Registrar.*"

(*Then follows a list of the names of all the Clergy cited.*)

The numbers of votes were sent to the Bishop, as an extra-official communication.*

Before I quit this subject, I may mention that the Bishops,

---

* The numbers were—Mr. Wilkinson 105, Mr. Cadman 100, Mr. Hodson 90, Mr. Fleming 82.

as a body, feel themselves committed to enlargement of the number of Proctors for the Parochial Clergy—of this the Bishop of London informed me some time ago. The Lawyers seem to be in the way of action. Some of them suggest that the assent of the Crown and of Parliament is necessary to sanction such a step. Some the assent of the Crown only. My belief is, that as Parliament has never meddled with Convocation,* and, in fact, is only a collateral institution with it, it would be suicidal to invite its aid; that if any external aid is required it is that of the Crown, but that really the determination of the matter rests with the Archbishop. This is evident from old alterations. The Archbishop, and the Archbishop only, has admitted Bishops of new Dioceses, and new Archdeacons of old Dioceses, and Proctors for Dioceses newly constituted. Surely these are structural alterations of great gravity in themselves and of great authority as precedents.

I do not enter at this time upon the consideration of any scheme for the infusion of the Lay element into Convocation, or of the creation of Lay Chambers which should be coordinate with it. I have given you in a former year my reasons for thinking that the former proposal would utterly change the constitution of Convocation, and destroy its *préstige* as an Institution at least coeval with Parliament, and that the latter would be cumbrous and unworkable.

---

* I quote the following from Dr. Trevor's *Convocations of the Two Provinces*:—"Neither William of Orange, nor his English advisers, had much respect for the clerical function. But on the introduction of a Bill into Parliament for the comprehension of Dissenters within the English Establishment, both Houses demurred, and addressed the Crown, that, according to the ancient practice, and usage of this Kingdom in time of Parliament, His Majesty would be graciously pleased to issue forth his writs, as soon as conveniently might be, for calling a Convocation of the Clergy of this Kingdom to be advised with touching Ecclesiastical matters." This seems to show that Parliament had no jealousy of Convocation, that it recognized its position in the Constitution, and desired that its advice should be had on such things as fell specially within its province.

## VIII.

I wish, however, to assure you that another Institution, the adoption of which I have earnestly urged upon you, that of a Diocesan Conference, by which I believe Clergy and Laity united may be brought *en rapport* with Convocation, has not ceased to interest me.

The Bishop, having had laid before him the results of my appeal to the Rural Deaneries in 1878, held a meeting of Archdeacons and Rural Deans in the Autumn of that year. A long discussion took place, in which various provisions of the proposed scheme were subjected to keen criticism. The Bishop then appointed a Committee, consisting of Canon Nisbet, Mr. Capel Cure, and myself, to reconsider and report especially upon the due Representation of the Laity, which, in his opinion, was the main difficulty. The Committee made a Report on that subject in June last to his Lordship, and also on the subject of Clerical Representation.* These the Bishop, in his Charge, commended to the careful consideration of the Rural Deaneries, saying that he was not unwilling to carry out their wishes, but that he wished to have their matured views. The Reports of the Rural Deaneries have been sent in, and his Lordship is still weighing the matter.

I trust that the result may be the establishment of a Diocesan Conference in our Diocese. It is one of the only three in the Province of Canterbury which, by the beginning of next year, will be without such an organization. The Dioceses of St. David's, Hereford, and Rochester will possess it in the course of this or the next year. In the Province of York every Diocese, (including that of Sodor and Man,) has set one on foot, with the exception of Durham; this, however, has announced one for September 21st and 22nd. In the whole

---

* *See* Appendix, pages 43, seqq.

c 2

of England and Wales, London, Llandaff, and Worcester will be the only Dioceses without it.

Perhaps I may mention that in the last group of Sessions of the late Convocation of Canterbury, a Committee was unanimously appointed to receive the Official Reports of the several Diocesan Conferences within the Province, and make such Report from time to time to the House upon the matter of such Reports as might be deemed desirable. I have the honour of being the Chairman of that Committee. Its Report is nearly ready, and I think will be found to possess much interest, though [it has been compiled under some disadvantages, and has involved some practical difficulty. Diocesan Conferences are, as a whole, a new institution. In some cases they have been established so recently as hardly to have assumed such form and working order as will bear analysis.

For instance—

Though, in *some* Dioceses, Resolutions have been passed, and carried into effect by means of diligent Committees, which have produced tangible results,

In *others*, Resolutions have been simply carried.

In *others*, Papers have been read without discussion.

In *others*, discussions have been raised without Resolutions being passed.

In *others*, attention has been merely drawn to wants, *gravamina*, or defects, no general discussion having ensued.

In *others*, the matters under discussion have been chiefly the constitution or reorganization of the Conference itself.

This diversity of circumstances or of procedure has, of course, rendered the Report of the Committee more unsystematic and fragmentary than it might otherwise have been. But, it is believed, the very exhibition of what may, without disrespect, be termed the tentative efforts of Diocesan Conferences, will suggest, both to those already formed, and to those which may hereafter be formed, the desirableness of method, and also of simultaneous discussion of the same subjects.

Fragmentary and unsystematic as it is, the Report will show how many important subjects are at this time, and have been for some time past, stirring the minds of those representative assemblages of Clergy and Laity, and, in many instances, the exact direction which their minds have taken.

## IX.

Since I last addressed you, in this place, an important event has occurred, the appointment of a Suffragan Bishop of London, under the Act of Henry the Eighth, by the title of Bishop of Bedford. He is concerned, as you know, with the Eastern part only of the Diocese, and it may perhaps be supposed for a moment that we are comparatively little concerned with the matter. Really we are deeply concerned. Whatever relieves the hands of our overworked Diocesan, and enables him to give greater attention to the rest of his charge, must be an advantage to us. Then, on the theory that a body, like a rope, is no stronger than it is at its weakest point, the whole Church of the Diocese must be the stronger if the Church, in this confessedly weak part of it, is raised in its tone, and made more felt by the population. Such, I believe, will under God's blessing, be the result of Bishop How's Missionary exertions—Missionary they must be, as all who know the difficulties, the discouragements, the sickness of heart, under which the East End Clergy are labouring, are very painfully aware.

And here would come in a third reason for our taking interest in this movement. It has long been my own feeling, and I know that a similar feeling has been entertained by others, that a Bishop in the East of London must be comparatively powerless unless he is aided by money, and by men—Presbyters, in the words of St. Ignatius, attached to the Bishop as strings to the harp—in fact, a personal staff, the members of which he may send, for a shorter or longer period, to help in the feebler Parishes, or to plant Mission Chapels in aid of the Incumbents. And money also, by which he may provide both for the maintenance of these men, and for the establishment of the many Parochial Agencies which richer Parishes enjoy. Can we not, ought we not, to help him, and that systematically and liberally, to meet what he must feel is a great and overwhelming necessity? I know indeed that some of the rich Parishes of the West have, in some cases for years, affiliated each a particular Eastern Parish, and sent pecuniary aid to it. I know that some send aid to many, every year. I know that Christian men and Christian women have, in various instances, devoted themselves, and their lives, to working in the East. But has not the hour arrived when, and has not the Bishop been appointed under whom, these desultory efforts may with advantage be systematized? Are we to go on contented with waging a guerilla warfare with evil, here and there only, where we hear of some great want, instead of moving, like a well-disciplined and consolidated army, under a competent commander? The former style of action is, to my mind, painfully like that condemned by the Athenian orator many years ago:—ὥσπερ οἱ βάρβαροι πυκτεύϑσιν, ὅτω πολεμεῖτε Φιλίππῳ· καὶ γὰρ ἐκείνων ὁ πληγεὶς, ἀεὶ τῆς πληγῆς ἔχεται· κἂν ἑτέρωσε πατάξῃ τις, ἐκεῖσέ εἰσιν αἱ χεῖρες· προβάλλεσθαι δὲ, ἢ βλέπειν ἐναντίον, ὅτε οἶδεν, ὅτ᾽ ἐθέλει. κ. τ. λ. This passage may be read at length in the 14th Chapter of the First Philippic of Demosthenes. May we not support on system some well-considered scheme such as I understand that the Bishop of Bedford is preparing, under the title of the *East London Church Society*, in order to help him in his work? His plans are not yet entirely matured, but they are on a most comprehensive scale. The clergy of the more opulent West-End Parishes might advance it,

1st. By having periodical collections in their Churches

to form a Fund, to be administered at the discretion of the Bishop of Bedford.

*2nd.* By devoting themselves, or some of their more active Curates, occasionally, to personal Missions in Parishes indicated by the Bishop, as in special need of such stirrings towards spiritual life.

*3rd.* By exciting their individual Parishioners, men and women alike, to employ themselves in the work of district visiting, or holding Mothers' Meetings, or giving evening instruction, with regularity and unity of purpose, in connection, of course, with the Incumbent, and beyond him, of the Bishop.

I have no Parish myself, but I should be very glad to do what I could, and to present a Donation of Fifty Pounds in furtherance of this evangelizing design.

I have said already, the money has been in many instances given. But its bestowers have confessed themselves scarcely satisfied with the results. In neighbouring Parishes, perhaps equally necessitous, it has produced discontent; and being lavished on one Parish in particular, it has produced demoralisation and abandonment of efforts at self-help.

As to the second point. Special Missions have taken place. But the effect has been transient, because the movement has been transient, and like the memory of a guest who abideth but for a day.

As to the third point. Experience has already shown the blessings both to the giver and to the receiver of such efforts. But a succession of persons is wanted, and a system which shall permeate the whole of the dreary waste which lies eastward of London Bridge.

I have already spoken on the subject to various of the West End Clergy; and I trust that when the Bishop of Bedford's plans are matured, and he is able to take a conspectus of his territory, some plan like that which is here only indicated may be brought to bear. I am sure that our own sympathies, and I am sure that the sympathies of many of the Laity, are already with our brethren in the East. Of course there are Parishes in our own Archdeaconry in similar need. They also should be helped. But as a general rule, we have reason to thank God that we are generally better off, and in a condition to argue thus with ourselves: How wretched should we be, were our own Churches empty, if we found it impossible to get assistance in our Services; and in our Parochial works, how much should we miss that band of lay-helpers who collect and contribute to our offertories, or those faithful women who visit our poor districts, and gather our young female Communicants and guard them kindly! Contrast with this the lot of a Clergyman, perhaps with no Curate to help him, in the care of five or ten thousand people, and those five or ten thousand, not only not rich, but consisting of families not one of which is able to keep a servant, and with a Church, squalid and destitute of worshippers, devoid of warmth and life, materially and spiritually. I know not how, if we shut our eyes and our ears to all this, we can avoid a humiliating self-application of the text, " Whoso hath this world's goods, and seeth his brother have need, and shutteth up his compassion for him, how dwelleth the love of God in him? "

## X.

I have detained you, my Brethren, already longer than I should have wished to do; and, after all, I fear I have set forth some of the topics on which I have enlarged with a feebleness utterly disproportioned to the weight with which I find them pressing upon myself. Forgive me, if I say a very few words more on a subject which has given me some disquietude. I mean what I cannot help calling an unnatural alliance between the secularizers of the Lord's Day, who would allow all sorts of public lectures to be given and all sorts of exhibitions to be opened upon it, as being no better than other days, and certain of our zealous Clergy, who would wish exhibitions to be open, for the following reason. They find it almost hopeless, they say, to wean many of the lower classes from the public-house, and bring them out of their degrading associations, by religious attractions. Therefore they will try what at any rate are humanizing influences, hoping for better things bye and bye.

While I object to unnecessary interference with the employments of persons on the Lord's Day; while I press that it was intended for the rest of the body as well as for the rest and improvement of the soul; while I would promote enjoyment of all by parks and open spaces, I earnestly deprecate such an alliance,

1*stly*. Intellectual tastes cannot be implanted at once, and their objects would not engage the classes intended.

2*ndly*. Opening places of exhibitions would lead to opening other places, such as theatres, which would utterly secularize the Holy Day.

3*rdly*. The attraction of such opening would be a snare to many who at present devote the Lord's Day, more or less, to religious purposes, and who are contented with the parks and wholesome out-door recreations.

On these grounds, among others, I entreat you pause before you join in such a movement. I respect the intentions of those of my Brethren who have already joined in it; but I am sure they are mistaken, and I believe they will be sadly disappointed.

———

You will not have expected me to treat upon political topics, though a change has just taken place in the Government which some persons imagine may injuriously affect the interests of the Church. I have not the slightest fear (so long as she is true to herself) for the interests of the Church even as an Establishment. No Statesman wantonly assails or tears to pieces an Institution, the growth of Centuries, to which he is personally attached, or which he cannot help confessing to be doing incalculable good. The chiefs of those who are now called to the helm of affairs come under the one or the other of these categories. The eloquent Premier, who, only eleven months ago, in advocating the Additional Curates Society, said, "I believe that we who are here assembled, and that thousands and thousands and tens of thousands and millions outside these walls, are united in the firm conviction that the Church of England has still a great work to perform for herself, for the people and for Christendom at large:" The son of that great territorial Duke, who is the Chancellor of the University of Cambridge, who has munificently subscribed towards the Bishopric of Southwell, and who has built I know not how many Churches for the benefit of his dependents, and for the glory of God: The high-minded lawyer who, no long time since, declined aggrandisement lest it should involve him in action against the Irish Church: And the religious Nonconformist who said that though not agreeing with her, he acknowledged the benefits which the Church of England conferred upon the Nation, and would not join in a cry against her—These are not men to be feared. And if they were, the Church is day by day becoming stronger in her temporal position, because she is day by day increasingly in earnest in her work. Her motto is *Laborare et orare*, and she puts forth the first of these, to her, inseparable, energies, in the Divine strength obtained by the second. So, *finally*, Let us humbly beseech our Heavenly Father, that His continual pity may cleanse and defend His Church, and that, because it cannot continue in safety without His succour, He may preserve it evermore by His help and goodness through Jesus Christ our Lord. AMEN.

43

# APPENDIX.

### Note to page 24.

St. Alban's and Rochester are, I think, the only Dioceses in which a custom like that in the Diocese of London prevails, namely, of the Bishop's selecting two from the Procurators elected by the Archdeaconries. Curiously enough, the custom was imported thither from London. Rochester had formerly only one Archdeacon whose title was Archdeacon of Rochester, and two Procurators were elected under his presidency for the Diocese. When, in 1838, the Archdeaconries of Essex, Colchester, and St. Alban's were transferred from the Diocese of London to Rochester, and the Archdeaconries of Rochester and St. Alban's were united in one person, the following arrangement took place :—Each of the then three Archdeaconries elected *two* Proctors, and the Bishop following the London custom, selected at his pleasure two out of the six. On the formation of the Diocese of St. Alban's, three Archdeaconries were taken from Rochester, viz., Essex, Colchester, and St. Alban's, and these three elected two Procurators each, or six in the whole, out of whom the Bishop selected two. As for Rochester, it retained the Archdeaconry of Rochester, and had two new Archdeaconries created, those of Southwark and Kingston-upon-Thames. Each of these Archdeaconries now elects two Procurators, and the Bishop selects two out of the six submitted to him. He has done his best for the Clergy, by appointing one Procurator to represent the County of Kent, and another to represent the County of Surrey. The Bishop of St. Alban's has simply exercised his old prerogative, feeling no doubt the impossibility of complying with the Archbishop's suggestion.

### (See page 35.)

REPORT OF COMMITTEE ON THE ELECTION OF LAY REPRESENTATIVES AT A DIOCESAN CONFERENCE FOR THE DIOCESE OF LONDON.

At a Meeting held at the house of the ARCHDEACON OF MIDDLESEX, on Friday, June 13th, 1879 :—

Present :—The Venerable the ARCHDEACON, the Rev. E. CAPEL CURE and the Rev. CANON NISBET, two of the Rural Deans, who had been nominated by the BISHOP OF LONDON as a Committee to report upon the above matter :—

The Rules of eight Diocesan Conferences (viz.: Chichester, Lichfield, Manchester, Norwich, Oxford, Ripon, Salisbury, Winchester) were carefully examined, and it was found that the mode of Election of the Lay Members of such Conferences is *almost identical in the several Dioceses, and very similar* to the plan sketched out by the Archdeacon in his recent Charge (page 36).

That ordinarily *two* Meetings are held.

*First*, a Meeting of Male Adult Members of the Church of England, of each Parish, summoned by the Incumbent, for the purpose of electing two Delegates (being Communicants) to attend a subsequent Meeting convened by the Rural Dean.

*Second*, a Meeting of such Delegates convened in each Rural Deanery, by the Rural Dean, for the purpose of electing Representatives of the Deanery at the Conference according to the number allotted to the Deanery.

The Representatives in all cases are Communicants, and their number is determined on the basis of the number of Parishes in each Deanery, qualified to a certain extent by the amount of population and general circumstances of the Deanery.

Having regard to the precedents thus furnished by the practice of eight Dioceses, It was resolved, in the event of a Diocesan Conference being held in the Diocese of London, to recommend that the mode of election of Lay Representatives at the Conference should be as follows :—

In every Parish, all Laymen, Members of the Church of England, of full age, resident in the Parish, or worshipping at any one of the Churches or Chapels in the Parish, shall be summoned, as often as may be necessary, by the Incumbent and Churchwardens (or one of them), to a Meeting, for the purpose of electing, by a majority of the persons present thereat, two Laymen who shall be called Parish Delegates.

Notice of such Meeting shall be given on the preceding Sunday orally by the Minister during the time of Divine Service, in every Church of England Place of Worship in the Parish, and also by a paper affixed by the Minister and Churchwardens to the doors of every such Place of Worship.

The Lay Members of Conference shall be elected by these Parish Delegates at a Meeting summoned by the Rural Dean. For the purpose of these Rules the word Parish means an *Ecclesiastical* Parish or District.

The election of Members of Conference at the Meetings summoned by the Rural Dean shall be by voting papers, each Voter having as many votes as there are Members to be elected, which votes may be distributed or given cumulatively, at the will of the Voter. But the voting papers of persons not present at the Meeting shall not be taken into account, unless the cause of their absence be allowed by the Meeting.

Both Parish Delegates and Members of Conference shall be elected triennially; vacancies to be filled up when necessary at intermediate Meetings, summoned as above.

The Forms for the election of Lay Members which are given below are recommended for adoption.

With regard to the number of Representatives from each Deanery in the Diocese of London the following method is recommended :—

1.—That there should be no official Lay Representatives, and that the Representatives should not be necessarily inhabitants of the Deanery.

2.—That, there being a large number of Deaneries (25), there should be not less than 200 Lay Representatives, which would give an average of 8 to each Rural Deanery.

3.—But that, in assigning the number of Representatives to each, regard should be had not merely to the population of the Deaneries but to the circumstances of the various localities.

The following Schedule has been drawn up on two different plans with nearly the same result—in the one case 205 Members, in the other 204.

The first plan was to give 5 Members to each Deanery, making a total of 125, and adding 10 Members to Kensington, Marylebone, Paddington, St. Pancras, St. George, Hanover Square, Islington and Stepney (a total of 70), making 195, and then 5 additional Members to Hackney and to Spitalfields, making a complete total of 205.

The other process was the adoption of a general principle—to give five Members to each Deanery which had a population of not less than 50,000 and not more than 100,000, and that in those Deaneries where the population was more than 100,000 there should be five Representatives for each 50,000—with some slight alterations in regard of a few exceptional Deaneries (such as Stepney, which has a population of 320,000.) The total arrived at by this method is shown to be 204.

SCHEDULE.

| DEANERIES. | PARISHES. | POPULATION. | REPRESENTATIVES. | |
|---|---|---|---|---|
| | | | PLAN 1. | PLAN 2. |
| Fulham ... | 12 | 70,000 | 5 | 5 |
| Kensington ... | 30 | 130,000 | 5+10 | 15 |
| Bloomsbury ... | 2 | 53,000 | 5 | 5 |
| Chelsea ... | 8 | 72,000 | 5 | 5 |
| Ealing ... | 30 | 70,000 | 5 | 5 |
| Enfield ... | 20 | 70,000 | 5 | 5 |
| St. George, Hanover Square | 10 | 90,000 | 5+10 | 10 |
| Hampton ... | 18 | 50,000 | 5 | 5 |
| Harrow ... | 19 | 40,000 | 5 | 5 |
| Highgate ... | 20 | 60,000 | 5 | 5 |
| St. Martin ... | 8 | 60,000 | 5 | 5 |
| Marylebone ... | 20 | 160,000 | 5+10 | 15 |
| Paddington ... | 20 | 100,000 | 5+10 | 10 |
| St. Pancras ... | 27 | 225,000 | 5+10 | 15 |
| Uxbridge ... | 13 | 25,000 | 5 | 3 |
| St. James ... | 5 | 30,000 | 5 | 5 |
| St. Margaret, Westminster | 11 | 60,000 | 5 | 5 |
| East City ... | 25 | 25,000 | 5 | 3 |
| West City ... | 40 | 35,000 | 5 | 3 |
| Hackney ... | 22 | 150,000 | 5+5 | 15 |
| Islington ... | 35 | 240,000 | 5+10 | 15 |
| St. Sepulchre ... | 22 | 160,000 | 5 | 10 |
| Shoreditch ... | 20 | 135,000 | 5 | 10 |
| Spitalfields ... | 25 | 196,000 | 5+5 | 10 |
| Stepney ... | 40 | 320,000 | 5+10 | 15 |
| | | | 205 | 204 |

(*Forms to be used in Election of Lay Members.*)

**Form A.**

LONDON DIOCESAN CONFERENCE.

*Letter of the Bishop to Incumbent and Churchwardens.*

GENTLEMEN, Fulham Palace, 187 .

In accordance with the Constitution of the London Diocesan Conference, I have to request you to call a Meeting of the Adult Male Members of the Church of England resident in your Parish, for the purpose of electing two Laymen, being Communicants, to vote, as Parish Delegates, on behalf of

the Parish, for the Lay Representatives of the Rural Deanery in which
your Parish is situate, at the Diocesan Conference to be held at
on the      and      of      , 187 .

Notices to be affixed to the Church door (Form B) are sent herewith.

The Incumbent, or on his failure (as hereafter mentioned) one of the
Churchwardens, will preside at the aforesaid Parish Meeting, and is par-
ticularly requested to forward to the Rural Dean, on or before the
day of      next, the names and addresses of the two Laymen who
are elected, in order that the Rural Dean may summon them to a Meeting
at some convenient place where they shall proceed to elect Representatives
to the Conference for the Deanery.

A copy of this letter has also been this day sent to the Churchwardens in
a separate envelope, and they are requested and authorised to summon the
Parochial Meeting on the failure of the Incumbent to do so, within twenty-
one days from the receipt of this letter.

I am, dear Sir,<br>Yours very faithfully,

*To the Incumbent and*
*Churchwardens of the Parish of*

---

**Form B.**

LONDON DIOCESAN CONFERENCE.

NOTICE TO BE AFFIXED TO THE CHURCH DOORS.

TAKE NOTICE, that all Adult Male Members of the Church of England,
resident in this Parish, are requested to attend a Meeting, which will be
held in      on      , the
day of      , at      o'clock, for the purpose of
choosing two Laymen, being Communicants, as Parochial Delegates, to vote
on behalf of the Parish for the Lay Representatives of the Rural Deanery at
the Diocesan Conference.

Signature of the Incumbent, or of one, } <br>
    or both, of the Churchwardens. }

Dated      187 .

---

**Form C.**

LONDON DIOCESAN CONFERENCE.

*Letter from the Bishop to the Rural Deans.*

REV. AND DEAR SIR,      Fulham Palace, 187 .

I have requested the Incumbent and Churchwardens of each Parish in
your Deanery to return to you, not later than the      day of
     , the names and addresses of the two Parochial Delegates
chosen by each Parish. When you have received these returns, will you
be so good as to arrange for a Meeting of all the Parochial Delegates at a
convenient time and place, and then and there proceed to the election of
Lay Representatives to the Conference for the Deanery; a form of letter

(Form D), summoning the Parochial Electors to this Meeting, is sent herewith.

Immediately after this Meeting you are requested to send to
the Lay Secretary, a return of the names and addresses of the Laymen elected to be the Representatives of your Deanery at the Conference, their names being placed in order according to the number of votes given to each.

I am,

Yours very faithfully,

To

---

### Form D.

#### LONDON DIOCESAN CONFERENCE.

187 .

*Letter from the Rural Dean summoning the two Laymen chosen by every Parish in the Rural Deanery (otherwise called the Parochial Delegates) to a Meeting.*

DEAR SIR,

I beg to summon you to a Meeting of Parochial Delegates to be held at
on the day of next
at o'clock, for the purpose of proceeding to elect Representatives to the Diocesan Conference for this Rural Deanery.

I am, dear Sir,

Yours very faithfully,

*Rural Dean.*

To

#### INSTRUCTIONS.

The votes at the Meeting to which you are hereby summoned will be given on paper.

In case you should be unable to attend the Meeting, you may, if you think fit, give your written authority, to the other Parochial Delegate chosen by your Parish to vote on your behalf in the election of Lay Representatives, on his explaining the cause of your absence.

You are entitled to vote for Representatives for this Deanery, but you may give accumulative votes for the same person, to the extent of that number.

The Representatives must be Laymen, being Communicants of the Church of England and resident in the Diocese, but not necessarily in the Rural Deanery which they represent.

## Form E.

### LONDON DIOCESAN CONFERENCE.

#### RETURN MADE BY RURAL DEAN.

*Form of Return of Lay Representatives of the Deanery of*
*to be sent to the Lay Secretary of the Conference.*

I hereby certify that the highest number of votes for the
Lay Representatives of the above named Rural Deanery has been given to
the following persons—

| Names (in full). | Addresses. |
|---|---|
| | |

Signed, on behalf of the Committee,

J. A. HESSEY, D.C.L.,

*Archdeacon of Middlesex.*

---

## FURTHER REPORT OF COMMITTEE WITH REFERENCE TO A DIOCESAN CONFERENCE FOR THE DIOCESE OF LONDON.

MY LORD BISHOP,

Since our Report to you upon the Election of Lay Representatives we
have turned our attention to the manner in which Representatives of the
Clergy may be elected, the qualification of Electors, and the principles upon
which a certain number of Representatives may be assigned to each Rural
Deanery.

As to the manner, we think that there can be no difficulty in the Rural
Dean's appointing a day on which all the Beneficed Clergy, and Licensed
Incumbents of Proprietary Chapels, and such other Clergy as are hereafter
specified,* within his Deanery, may be assembled, and proceed to the Election
out of their own body, by signed voting papers, of such a number of
Representatives in the Conference as may be assigned to them.

Each Voter should have as many votes as there are Representatives to be
elected, and he should be permitted to distribute these votes, or to accumulate
them on one person.

We have carefully considered the limits within which the privilege of
voting should be conferred. After considerable hesitation we propose that
it be extended to all Curates in Priest's orders, who have been licensed in
the Diocese for not less than four years, or who have held your Lordship's
written permission to officiate for at least the same length of time. On the
one hand, we desire to avoid the prejudice that would hinder the working of

---

* The words "and such other Clergy as are hereafter specified," were, through an
oversight, omitted in the earlier impressions of this document.

the new Conference, if so large and influential a body of men as the Licensed Curates in your Lordship's Diocese felt themselves excluded from all share in its deliberations. On the other hand, we wish to secure for the Conference the widest possible range from which the Representatives should be selected. It is only by placing it on the firmest and broadest basis, when every Church interest is represented fully, and every Church work is enabled to obtain attention to its wants, that we can hope to gain for the proposed Diocesan Conference vitality and permanence.

On these grounds also we would suggest that Secretaries of Church Societies within the Diocese, in Priest's orders, if they have held for four years your Lordship's written permission to officiate, should have votes in the Rural Deaneries within which the offices of their Societies are respectively situate.

---

We now come to the principle upon which we think that Representatives should be assigned to each Rural Deanery. It is expressed in the following Schedule, of which we offer an explanation.

We have taken two as the smallest number for any Deanery.

We have then assumed the principle of one Representative for every four Parishes, qualifying it however, by having regard to the amount of the population and other circumstances connected with them : this has had the result, in some instances of lessening, and in others of increasing, the number of Representatives. (Thus Fulham is a fair case of three Representatives, there being 12 Parishes and 70,000 people. In the case of Hampton, with 18 Parishes, and only 50,000 people, the principle of one for every four must be modified by abatement. Whereas in that of St. George, Hanover Square, it must be modified by enlargement, as it includes several Proprietary Chapels, and as the constituent Parishes are important.)

For the sake of comparison we have reprinted the Schedule of Lay Representatives, and annexed to it that of the Clerical Representatives. It will be seen that on our plan the number of the former was to be 205 or 204. The number of the latter will be 102. To these, however, we should be disposed to add,

The Bishop Suffragan of Bedford.
The Dean of St. Paul's.
The Dean of Westminster.
The Archdeacon of London.
The Archdeacon of Middlesex.
The two Proctors representing St. Paul's and Westminster respectively.
The two Proctors representing the Parochial Clergy.
The Diocesan Inspector of Schools.

This would raise the Clerical element of the Conference to 112.

We were at first inclined to admit a larger number of Clergy to seats in the Conference in right of their official position. But we find that in most other Conferences this right has been gradually restricted to about the limit which we have now suggested. Objections to its wider adoption have been expressed in many of our own Rural Deaneries. And, it will be recollected, that we have forborne to recommend it at all, in reference to the Lay element.

| DEANERIES. | PARISHES. | POPULATION. | LAY REPRESENTATIVES. | | CLERICAL REPRESEN-TATIVES. |
|---|---|---|---|---|---|
| | | | PLAN 1. | PLAN 2. | PLAN. |
| Fulham ... ... ... | 12 | 70,000 | 5 | 5 | 3 |
| Kensington ... ... | 30 | 130,000 | 5+10 | 15 | 7 |
| Bloomsbury ... ... | 2 | 53,000 | 5 | 5 | 2 |
| Chelsea ... ... | 8 | 72,000 | 5 | 5 | 3 |
| Ealing ... ... ... | 30 | 70,000 | 5 | 5 | 5 |
| Enfield ... ... | 20 | 70,000 | 5 | 5 | 4 |
| St. George, Hanover Square | 10 | 90,000 | 5+10 | 10 | 4 |
| Hampton ... ... | 18 | 50,000 | 5 | 5 | 3 |
| Harrow ... ... | 19 | 40,000 | 5 | 5 | 3 |
| Highgate ... ... | 20 | 60,000 | 5 | 5 | 4 |
| St. Martin ... ... | 8 | 60,000 | 5 | 5 | 2 |
| Marylebone ... ... | 20 | 160,000 | 5+10 | 15 | 5 |
| Paddington ... ... | 20 | 100,000 | 5+10 | 10 | 5 |
| St. Pancras ... ... | 27 | 225,000 | 5+10 | 15 | 6 |
| Uxbridge ... ... | 13 | 25,000 | 5 | 3 | 2 |
| St. James ... ... | 5 | 30,000 | 5 | 5 | 2 |
| St. Margaret, Westminster | 11 | 60,000 | 5 | 5 | 2 |
| East City ... ... | 25 | 25,000 | 5 | 3 | 3 |
| West City ... ... | 40 | 35,000 | 5 | 3 | 4 |
| Hackney ... ... | 22 | 150,000 | 5+5 | 15 | 5 |
| Islington ... ... | 35 | 240,000 | 5+10 | 15 | 7 |
| St. Sepulchre ... | 22 | 160,000 | 5 | 10 | 4 |
| Shoreditch ... ... | 20 | 135,000 | 5 | 10 | 4 |
| Spitalfields ... ... | 25 | 196,000 | 5+5 | 10 | 5 |
| Stepney ... ... | 40 | 320,000 | 5+10 | 15 | 8 |
| | | | 205 | 204 | 102 |
| | | OFFICIAL REPRESENTATIVES | | ... | 10 |
| | | | | | 112 |

Thus the whole number of the Conference would be 317 or 316.

Signed, on behalf of the Committee,

J. A. HESSEY, D.C.L.,

*Archdeacon of Middlesex.*

To

THE LORD BISHOP OF LONDON.